ENJOYING
LIFE

Devotionals to help you find joy in life.

Joy Oguntimein

Copyright Page

www.pocketfulofjoy.com

Cover by Joy Oguntimein

ISBN: 9798573024950

DEDICATION

To women of color who want to make lemonade and margaritas as life throws them lemons. To those who had an idea and turned it into a reality, in 2020.

I pray these devotions draw you closer to God's presence. As you read an entry may you be encouraged to choose Jesus and choose joy no matter your circumstances.

ACKNOWLEDGMENTS

Thank you, God, for the idea and for making this happen.

Thank you to everyone who has prayed and supported me on this journey...from reading early drafts, to giving me advice on the cover, and to reminding me of the impact this devotional could have on so many people. Thank you.

Contents

Get the Most out of This Devotional

Ideally, a devotional book enhances your quiet time with Jesus. No devotional book should ever replace your reading the Bible and praying from the heart. Think of this devotional as an appetizer, preparing your heart for the main course: The Word of God.

While these devotionals are short, my prayer is that each entry is more than a check, in a box on my to-do list, but rather a tool God uses to check your heart and change your perspective. Read the whole chapter or at least the two verses before and two verses after the highlight scripture. Allow the Holy Spirit to give you insight, understanding, and context.

Here are tips for getting the most of each entry:

- **Open your quiet time with prayer.** Ask the Holy Spirit to speak truth to your heart. Pray for wisdom and understanding to apply what you glean in your life.

- **Read the daily Scripture from your Bible in its greater context.** Open your Bible, Bibleapp, or biblegateway.com. Read at least three verses before and three verses after the scripture. Read slowly. Allow the Holy Spirit to guide you as you interact more fully with the actual text so that you can apply it.

- **Journal your reflections on the passage.** While my spiritual insight can be helpful, do not let it get in the way of anything God wants to show you Himself. Record any insights, questions, direction, and application you have.

- **Reflect on the 'Joyful Truth'.** Each Joyful Truth is a takeaway to help you remember what you have read. You may have a different takeaway. Awesome! Based on the scripture and devotion, consider what you need to change to align

1

yourself with what God has revealed to you.

The Creator of the Universe wants to commune with us and reveal who He really is. He does this through his word that "will empower you by its instruction and correction, giving you the strength to take the right direction and lead you deeper into the path of godliness" (2 Timothy 3:16 TPT). His word is still "living and active. Sharper than any double-edged sword" (Hebrews 4:12 CEB). So, open his word so you can not only have joy, but also be perfectly prepared to fulfill any assignment God gives you.

Opportunity for Joy

Read: James 1:1-5

"My fellow believers, when it seems as though you are facing nothing but difficulties see it as an invaluable opportunity to experience the greatest joy that you can!" (James 1:2 TPT)

There are numerous articles and blog posts on how to turn around a bad day. You can pet a pet, give a hug, think happy thoughts, the list goes on. But what do you do when it is a rough month, year, or decade? What do you do when it is one of those "This sucks! This is the absolute worst! How did I get here? Why is this happening to me? I just want to curl up and cry!" seasons? The Bible, in James 1:2-4, gives us a wild idea for how to respond to trials—we are instructed to view trials and difficulties as an opportunity for joy.

Joy is more than a feeling. Joy is an attitude of the heart and spirit shaped by contentment, confidence, and hope. Because joy is more than an emotion, joy can coexist with other emotions such as sadness, shame or anger. Joy doesn't need a smile to be valid or authentic. This understanding of joy helps us to begin making sense of James' request to have a joy-filled perspective when responding to life's difficult situations. In the midst of despair, trials, and negative circumstances James asks believers to choose joy.

God can use struggles to build resilience in us, strengthen our resolve, and enhance our ability to endure.

Our trials are opportunities for great joy because they are opportunities for God to grow and mature us in our faith (James 1:3-4). God can use struggles to build resilience in us, strengthen our resolve, and enhance our ability to endure. Trials draw us closer to God, teach us to cling to Him, and enable us to reflect Jesus more accurately to a world that desperately needs Him. Our

Joyful Truth

God is in full control
and can work all
things for good
(Romans 8:28).

trials, though incredibly confusing and painful, initiate a process which deepens and matures our faith in a way nothing else can.

We can make an intentional decision to have joy based on our faith; our conviction of things we know will come but have not yet seen (Hebrews 11:1). That is what Jesus did. He focused on the future reward and endured the torture of the cross "for the joy set before Him" (Hebrews 12:2). He chose joy because He thought of how God would be glorified and how people would be saved through His obedience. Despite our adversities, we can have joy if we deliberately choose to pause and refocus on our faith in Jesus. Let us fix our eyes on Jesus, the pioneer and perfecter of faith, the One whom our faith depends on from beginning to end.

How do we get to a place where we can choose joy during the trial? We start by choosing joy daily. A top-notch athlete does not wait until the big game to start preparing to win. Every day she does something to prepare her mind and body to win the game. Choosing joy during a trial is no different. This world is broken, and hardship is unavoidable. We must start choosing joy now, so it is natural to choose joy when trials come.

If you're in the midst of a trial, be encouraged, friend. God promises to mature and complete you through it. He will give you the strength to endure difficulties and the faith to wait for His good purposes to be accomplished in you. Be assured, not only is He in full control, but He is also able to work all things for good (Romans 8:28). Don't give up, let Him finish His work in you!

Dear God, You know I do not like trials, troubles, suffering, or pain; but I understand they are part of life. Help me to "choose joy" during it all. Remind me during my suffering that Your plans for me are still good. Give me the courage to persevere so that You can mold me into who You created me to be. I thank you because through these hard times, You will bring about joy, perseverance, and maturity in me. Amen.

Reflect: What do you know about God's character that can help you choose joy, even in troubled times? What are some ways you can practice being joy-filled even when circumstances are tough?

_____
_____
_____
_____
_____
_____
_____
_____
_____
_____
_____
_____
_____
_____
_____
_____
_____
_____
_____
_____
_____
_____
_____
_____
_____
_____
_____
_____
_____
_____
_____
_____
_____
_____
_____

Joy of Being You

Read: Psalm 139: 13-18

"Thank you for making me so wonderfully complex!
Your workmanship is marvelous—how well I know it. "
Psalm 139:14 NLT

I do not know about you, but I have often found myself falling into the trap of assessing my worth based on what is present in other people's lives and apparently missing from mine. For a long time, I did this with my single status. Rather than discovering and embracing my own value, I compared myself to people on my Facebook feed who were in a relationship. Before I knew it, I was not just comparing myself to people who were in a relationship, I was comparing myself to others my age, comparing job titles, homeownership status, new car purchase, etc. This comparison stole my joy. Can you relate?

He uniquely and precisely created each of us with specific gifts and talents to do exactly what He has called us to do.

Comparison is one of the tools the devil uses to keep us from stepping into our God-given destinies. How? Comparison lures us into wasting our time and energy trying to accumulate "currency" in the form of money, accomplishments, appearances, status, connections, and other external things. The yearning to be like another person causes stress, pain, and confusion. However, being our authentic self is liberating, exciting, and fulfilling. How would our lives be better if instead of trying to be what we think we're supposed to be, we were just ourselves?

Beloved, let us stop being distracted by comparison and embrace our God-given uniqueness (Romans 12:6)! Recognizing what is true about who we are leads to praise; it fills us with new wonder and worship. Let us focus on how wonderfully marvelous we are, rather than our flaws, faults, and the perceived perfection of others on TV and/or social media. Let us remember our own uniqueness, purpose, identity, and worth. God does not need two people just alike. He uniquely and precisely created each of us with specific gifts and talents to do exactly what He has called us to do. Become the original, authentic you that God created you to be.

Joyful Truth

Speak these truths: I have worth. I have value. I am loved. I am a child of the King of Kings.

On days when we doubt our worth and feel "less than," let us remember this: God chose and loved us before we were created (Ephesians 1:4). He created us, looked at us, then gave us His stamp of approval. No matter the size, age, or agility of our body, we were created by an incredible, awe-inspiring Creator who designed us just the way we are, flaws and all. We are special. We are one-of-a-kind, and we have been created with an extraordinary purpose. Let us speak these truths over ourselves: I have worth. I have value. I am loved. I am a child of the King of Kings.

Let us experience joy by praising God, loving ourselves, taking care of ourselves, and being who God made us to be. When we love who we are, we develop confidence, courage, peace, and happiness. I will be me; you should be you. Each of us has a purpose that no one who has ever lived or will live can possibly fulfill. We are not accidents. We are wonderfully and fearfully made, by God, on purpose, for his purpose.

You were born to shine. Know that full well and be joyful.

Dear Great Creator, I am grateful you find value in me. Thank you for giving me worth in your eyes. Help me live as the one you uniquely intended me to be. Help me to love myself and be who you created me to be. Remind me that I am your masterpiece. Amen.

Reflect: What is unique about you? What do you love about
yourself?

_____
_____
_____
_____
_____
_____
_____
_____
_____
_____
_____
_____
_____
_____
_____
_____
_____
_____
_____
_____
_____
_____
_____
_____
_____
_____
_____
_____
_____
_____
_____
_____
_____
_____
_____
_____
_____

Joy of Peace

Read: Proverbs 12:13-20

"Deception fills the hearts of those who plot harm, but those who plan for peace are filled with joy."
Proverbs 12:20 TPT

What do you do when your family member says something hurtful to you? Or when people at church gossip about you? Or when a friend embarrasses you in public? As humans, our initial reaction is to plan some type of payback. (If you are an over-saved petty Betty, you probably pray for payback. You pray "Lord, you know what _____ did was wrong. Let something bad, but not too bad, happen to them.") Though our tendency may be to choose vengeance, God calls us to be peacemakers and to make every effort to live in peace with everyone (Romans 12:18, Hebrews 12:14).

Living in peace does not mean we have to agree with everyone's opinions or beliefs, condone people's behaviors, or belittle our perspectives or feelings. It means we surrender our ego and pride; so, we are willing to admit our wrongs, to apologize, to make things right, and to forgive. When we discuss an issue, we are cordial and respectful, seeking to understand, educate, and at times, agree

> Planning for peace does not mean we pointlessly try to avoid conflict but rather intentionally deal with conflict and aim to restore relationships (Romans 14:19).

to disagree with grace, mercy, and integrity. Planning for peace does not mean we pointlessly try to avoid conflict or attempt to appease everyone, but rather we intentionally deal with conflict and aim to restore relationships (Romans 14:19). We can experience joy when we address and resolve conflict in ways that promote peace.

Choose Joy

The Holy Spirit will help us determine what's best for us to do.

Many versions of Romans 12:18 such as NIV or NKJV start with "If." The word "if" implies there may be times when we may 'make every effort' and 'do [our] best' to 'pursue peace' and are unable to be at peace with someone. And that is okay. God asks that as much as it depends on us, allow peace to reign and Christ to be seen. We do our part and let him handle the rest. There may not be a happy outcome, but God will be glorified.

We must learn to be peacemakers if we are going to represent God (Matthew 5:9). In each relationship, peace will look differently. It may mean seeking reconciliation, seeking resolution, expressing emotions, not starting an argument, not provoking, pushing buttons, or keeping quiet. The Holy Spirit will help us determine what is best for us to do. The time and effort we put into cultivating peace contribute to the joy and fulfillment we have in life. Let us rely on the Holy Spirit to help us deal with our own heart so that we can be at peace with others.

Dear God, help me to choose peace and conflict resolution over payback and vengeance. By Your grace help me to live peaceably with others. Let me always remember that You have called me to be a peacemaker. Vengeance is Yours not mine. Amen.

Reflect: Who do you need to reconcile with today?

Joy of Trust

Read: Romans 15:8-14

"Now may God, the inspiration and fountain of hope, fill you to overflowing with uncontainable joy and perfect peace as you trust in him. And may the power of the Holy Spirit continually surround your life with his super-abundance until you radiate with hope!"
Romans 15:13 TPT

"NO! NO!" I screamed. It did not help. Not one bit. My brilliant solution for unclogging my toilet accomplished exactly the opposite of what I had intended. I stood helplessly as water and crap (literally) overflowed onto my bathroom floor. I tried fixing this problem on my own rather than seeking help. I did not ask my dad, ask a friend, or even the great wiz, Google, about how to unclog my toilet. I tried to fix this on my own, which led to a bigger mess. My response to my clogged toilet was similar to what happens when we try to control and contain the situations in our lives, rather than asking God for help and trusting him to come through.

Trust creates room for joy as we give our cares to the One who is in control and cares for us (1 Peter 5:7).

Raise your hand if you find this incredibly difficult to do despite knowing how awesome God is? I really hope I am not the only one raising my hand right now. Letting go of control and trusting Jesus is the core of the Christian life. Yet, in situations both the large and small, we find this incredibly difficult. Why? If we each made a list of our reasons why we find it difficult to trust God, some common themes may include fear, worry, past disappointments, and a distorted image of God. All these barriers steal our joy, affect the mind, and wound our physical wellness. Trust, however, creates room for joy, peace, and hope as we give our anxiety, concerns, and stresses to the One who is not only in control, but has promised to care for us (1 Peter 5:7; Psalm 94:19).

We can trust God and His goodness above all else. Why? Because He has consistently proven Himself faithful (Psalm 145:3). Every time the mind wanders toward worry or fear, let us pause and make an intentional choice to meditate on this defining quality of God. He is a faithful promise keeper who can be trusted. God knows what is going on in my life and your life. He knows all our needs and is never caught by surprise. God is a loving, trustworthy father and shepherd. He has, is, and will always take care of us. We can trust Him, always, this includes in the midst of a pandemic, racial injustice, job loss, & illness...pretty much all of what 2020 has brought us. Treasure this truth in your heart for those moments when you feel like your life is overflowing with crap.

> ## Choose Joy
>
> God is a loving, trustworthy father and shepherd. He is, was, and will always take care of us.

To fully experience God's blessings and promises, we must learn to trust God. This does not happen overnight, but gradually. Trust grows as we get to know God and realize for ourselves that He is both faithful and good. Dig into Scripture. Acquaint yourself with the promises of God and with His track record. He has a history of being faithful. Get to know the character of God and your joy, peace, hope, and willingness to trust in him will abound.

Dear God, Give me peace and joy as I trust you today. I know You care God and will take care of me and meet my needs, even when I can't see or feel it. Remind me that You are the God of the impossible. You can do anything. I trust in Your ability and not my own. Amen.

Reflect: When is it most difficult for you to trust God? What will you do today to build your trust in God?

_____

_____

_____

_____

_____

_____

_____

_____

_____

_____

_____

_____

_____

_____

_____

_____

_____

_____

_____

_____

_____

_____

_____

_____

_____

_____

_____

_____

_____

_____

_____

_____

_____

Joy of Redemption

Read: Psalm 71:20-24

"My lips will shout for joy when I sing praise to You—I, whom You have redeemed. "
Psalm 71:23 NIV

In the movie "Taken," retired CIA agent, Bryan Mills, travels across Europe and goes to great lengths to save his daughter, who has been kidnapped while on a trip to Paris. He spares nothing in his pursuit to find and save his daughter. Mills does everything possible and necessary to rescue his daughter. Similarly, God did the one thing necessary to rescue us. God gave his only son, Jesus, as the sacrifice to pay the debt for our sins and set us free.

Redemption is synonymous with being liberated, freed, or rescued from bondage and slavery to a person or thing. From the beginning, God has had a rescue plan, a redemption plan in place for us. Redemption is an act of God's grace, by which he rescues and restores us, through the work of Jesus on the cross. It is something

God "sent his Son . . . to redeem" us, so "that we might receive adoption to sonship" (Galatians 4:4-5).

He does to and for us so we can have a loving relationship with Him. God "sent his Son . . . to redeem" us, so "that we might receive adoption to sonship" (Galatians 4:4-5). Did you catch that? A relationship with you matters so much to God that he sacrificed his only son! You matter!

Redemption centers on the freedom Christ has secured for us that allows us to fully pursue a relationship with God. We are freed from the power of the grave (Psalm 49:15), from death (Hosea 13:14), from the law (Galatians 4:5), from all wickedness (Titus 2:14), from the curse (Galatians 3:13), from sin (Colossians 1:14) and from the pit (Psalm 103:4). Christ frees us to live a new life in Him. He has freed our soul

Choose Joy

and that is cause for praise (Psalm 71:23). Hallelujah!!!!!!!!!!!

His redemptive love is working in and through us, changing us, and making us more like Him.

We can be joyful knowing we are forgiven and free. God has redeemed us, and His redemptive love is working in and through us, changing us, and making us more like Him. We need to forgive ourselves, love ourselves, and accept the freedom that God's redemption brings.

Dear God, Thank you Lord for redeeming me. I'm grateful you are not limited by anything at all – even my sins – in accomplishing Your plans for me. Help me to embrace your redemptive love. Amen.

Reflect: Think about this phrase and write any responses that come to mind: "Redemption is not just for freedom; redemption is for a relationship with the Redeemer."

Joy of Generosity

Read: Psalm 41:1-3

"Oh, the joys of those who are kind to the poor! The LORD rescues them when they are in trouble. "
Psalm 41:1 NLT

She gave me her scarf?!? I was stunned. After a presentation, at an affordable housing conference, a lady living in public housing gave me the scarf off her neck simply because she loved my personality, loved bargain shopping, and loved to give. I was amazed at her generosity, amazed at how she joyfully gave. It was October. Fall was in the air and winter was coming; yet she gave me her scarf! Ms. Pat taught me that generosity is a heart thing, not a money thing.

Generous giving is more about the heart and spirit of our generosity than it is what we give. Whether we are giving our money, service, talents, or time, we should give generously. We should be like an overflowing river, not a dead sea. Giving generously allows us to be a

vessel for God's blessings and a reflection of Him. When we give generously, we demonstrate our confidence in God's provision for us. We demonstrate that we believe God is our Great Provider who is always ready to supply all we need (Philippians 4:19). When we give generously, to others, joy is ours and God is glorified. That is a double win!

> Giving generously allows us to be a vessel for God's blessings and a reflection of Him.

We can experience joy by being a blessing to others. Jesus said, "It is more blessed [and brings greater joy] to give than to receive." (Acts 20:35 AMP). Giving creates more room for peace, joy, and love. Here is a truth I am learning. No matter how big or small, the blessing God gives us it is never just for us. God blesses us so we can bless others. Even when times are tough, there is still an opportunity to be generous. What may seem little to us, may be great to someone else. When we give God whatever we have, (however small it may be), He multiplies it and does more with it than we can imagine. Let us freely live in obedience to Christ and be generous. We can trust God to keep His promises to bless us when we are generous (2 Corinthians 9:6-8). God is incredibly generous, and we can never outgive him (Luke 6:38). When we give to others or pour into the lives of others, God is standing by ready to fill us up.

Joyful Truths

When we give generously to others, joy is ours and God is glorified.

If you could use a joy boost, here is a suggestion: generously bless someone else. Do not limit your blessing to money. There are various ways to be a blessing. Encourage a co-worker. Help a struggling friend. Minister to a homeless person. God delights in our generosity. Our generosity for others reflects his loving heart toward us.

Dear God, Thank you for your generosity towards me. Teach me to give generously. Let me be a blessing to others. You are not stingy towards me and I do not want to be stingy towards others. Whether I'm experiencing lack or abundance, I want to point people toward you with my generosity. Amen.

Reflect: Read Luke 6:38. What does this verse say to you about the relationship between giving and receiving from God?

_____

_____

_____

_____

_____

_____

_____

_____

_____

_____

_____

_____

_____

_____

_____

_____

_____

_____

_____

_____

_____

_____

_____

_____

_____

_____

_____

_____

_____

_____

Joy of Forgiveness

Read: Colossians 3:12-17

"Bear with each other and forgive one another if any of you has a grievance against someone. Forgive as the Lord forgave you."
Colossians 3:13 NIV

Let's go ahead and admit what we all know: Forgiveness is hard. When we are hurt by those we love and trust, the pain can run deep. We feel we have a right to get even and do not want to move on until we do.

I remember when a church member said some hurtful words to me. She attacked my character. Even after I told her that what she said was painful, she did not apologize. I thought I had forgiven her, but I did not realize I had not forgiven her until she asked me to help her with something. The hurt came back, and I did not want to help her, at all. Here I was 3 months after the incident, still stuck in that moment, stuck in the past about to allow hurt and resentment to determine my decisions rather than God. I used to think that the only people who struggled with unforgiveness were people who had terrible things happen to

Choosing to forgive invites God to accomplish beautiful works of healing in our lives and our relationships.

them, people who had their hearts broken. Truth is that the people who struggle with unforgiveness are...well, people. Humans, people like me, and maybe people like you. We all struggle with forgiveness at some point in our lives.

It can be hard enough to forgive someone when they apologize. It can be extremely difficult when the person never attempts to right the wrong or asks for forgiveness. What are we supposed to do if the person does not think they have said or done anything wrong? Or, worse, they know, but they do not care? We still forgive because God

God will give us the power to...release unforgiveness, grab hold of joy, and be free.

still requires us to forgive (Ephesians 4:32). God forgave, and still forgives us, even when we do not repent. When we choose to forgive, we are not condoning the offense, excusing the wrongs done to us, or minimizing our hurts. Rather, we are choosing to give up our right to get even and trusting God to judge. Choosing to forgive invites God to accomplish beautiful works of healing in our lives and our relationships. As we move forward in forgiveness, God deals with the person. He probes their conscience and stirs conviction.

The cost of unforgiveness is greater than the cost of forgiveness. Unforgiveness tends to cost us our peace. Unforgiveness weighs us down and depletes our mental and emotional energy. All our resentment and bitterness toward people who have hurt us is not going to change the past, but it could damage the future. Feeling bitter may even feel right, at least for a short time. Eventually, just like the pain, the bitterness runs deep and grows roots. Its roots absorb and store hurt, anger, hatred, and revenge in our hearts. Choosing forgiveness prevents a bitter root from taking root in your heart and growing. Forgiveness prevents us from being held hostage by pain so our heart and soul can move forward in healing and freedom.

Even when nothing within us feels like forgiving, we must make the choice to forgive and endure the process. See, forgiveness is a decision and a process made possible not just by determination but by coordination with God. We must ask God to give us the strength and grace to fight through the feelings of anger, hatred, and bitterness. He will give us the power to forgive and surrender our hurt to Him. When that seems impossible, when you feel like you cannot be gracious toward someone, remember one thing: the cross where Christ forgave you. Let us release unforgiveness, grab hold of joy, and be free.

Dear God, Thank You for forgiving me. God help me, by faith, to forgive those who've wronged me. Heal my wounds and set me free. I don't want to miss out on any of the blessings You have for me because of bitterness and a hardened heart. Let your love flow through me. Amen.

Reflect: How have you seen a lack of forgiveness impact your life? Why is it so important to make a distinction between forgiveness as a decision and forgiveness as a process?

_____

_____

_____

_____

_____

_____

_____

_____

_____

_____

_____

_____

_____

_____

_____

_____

_____

_____

_____

_____

_____

_____

_____

_____

_____

_____

_____

_____

_____

_____

_____

_____

_____

_____

_____

_____

_____

_____

Joy of Sabbath Rest

Read: Isaiah 58:9-14

"If you keep your feet from breaking the Sabbath and from doing as you please on my holy day...then you will find your joy in the Lord"
Isaiah 58:13-14 NIV

Have you ever left a gift unopened? Perhaps a birthday or Christmas gift? I have! On more occasions than I would like to admit I have left a gift unopened for months. (Please do not tell my friends. I do not want them to stop giving me gifts.) In fact, one time I opened a birthday gift almost two years after I received it. Sadly, when it comes to God's gift, that is what many are doing. They have left one of the greatest gifts –Sabbath Rest - unopened. The Sabbath is a gift because it is a day for enjoyment. God divinely created and ordained a Sabbath day of rest for us to draw near to Him and rest in His holy presence!

Did you know keeping the Sabbath is one of the ten commandments? Yes, God commands us to honor the Sabbath day; to pause at least once a week and connect with Him (Exodus 20:8-10, Leviticus 23:3, Deuteronomy 5:12-15). With high ambitions, demands, and obligations, many of us tend to ignore this command. We do 'one more thing' and keep pressing forward then wonder why we are physically, mentally, emotionally, and spiritually drained. Setting the Sabbath apart from the busyness of the rest of the week breeds

With the blessings that come with it, we should preserve the Sabbath, not just observe it.

physical, mental, and emotional health by allowing us the opportunity to reflect, recreate, and recharge. The Sabbath is a time to rediscover our joy in the Lord as we center our focus and attention on Him (Isaiah 58:13-14). With the blessings that come with it, we should preserve the Sabbath, not just observe it. While Sabbath rest looks different for people, in all forms, it is a time to pause and reassure

The Sabbath is a time to rediscover our joy in the Lord as we center our focus and attention on Him (Isaiah 58:13-14).

ourselves of God's sovereignty.

Be intentional about doing the things that strengthen your relationship with God. Without some planning, everyday can easily become busy. Plan the week with the Sabbath day in mind so that you have plenty of time to rest and worship. Run errands, clean your house, and get other tasks taken care of so that way, the Sabbath day really will feel separate and holy. Your Sabbath does not have to be Sunday, but it must be the day you connect with God in a special way. On your Sabbath, you can write in your journal, go for a walk, connect with loved ones, or spend extra time reading your Bible, worshipping, and praying.

When we honor the Sabbath, we are expressing our freedom in Christ. We demonstrate that we are redeemed children of God instead of slaves to the tyranny of urgent busyness and activity. When we rest, we are recognizing God is the sustainer (Psalm 54:4). We have joy when we rest because we are reminded God has it (whatever that 'it' is) in control (Psalm 116:7). Sabbath rest is an act of faith showing that we know we will be taken care of in the absence of our "doing." Sabbath is not only a deliverance from work, but a symbol of deliverance from our own works. For one day a week, let us pause business as usual and let God direct our day according to his rhythm, not ours. Allow him to reveal where our mind and heart need to be realigned with his will and way.

Honoring the Sabbath and resting is not a sign of weakness; it is a sign of respect and trust. The Sabbath is a gift, open and enjoy it.

Dear God, Thank you for the Sabbath. Help me exchange the guilt of rest for the gift of rest. I want to intentionally preserve space to hear Your voice and for You to reveal the places I'm off track. You are my delight and I find my joy, hope, and rest in You. Amen.

Reflect: What do you do on your Sabbath to worship, rest, and celebrate? How does not working and setting day aside for God bring glory to God and joy to you?

_____
_____
_____
_____
_____
_____
_____
_____
_____
_____
_____
_____
_____
_____
_____
_____
_____
_____
_____
_____
_____
_____
_____
_____
_____
_____
_____
_____
_____
_____
_____
_____
_____
_____
_____
_____
_____

Joy of Confession

Read 1 John 1:5-10

"If we confess our sins, He is faithful and just to forgive us our sins and to cleanse us from all unrighteousness."
1 John 1:9 NIV

Ask most children, and they will tell you: confessing feels good. Recently a friend of mine was telling me how her little boy came to her room late at night to tell her how he got in trouble at school. When she asked why he felt the need to come to her so late at night to confess, he said "because he couldn't handle the 'pressure' of keeping a secret." It was keeping him up. I am not quite sure what happens to us as we grow up, but we begin thinking that it is better to hide when we have done wrong rather than go to our Father and confess our mistakes.

We can experience great joy when we confess. Confessing relieves the pressure of shame and guilt, making room for freedom and hope. God is never shocked when we confess our sins. Our all-knowing, ever-present Father is ready to forgive instantly, completely, and freely. He meets our confessions with grace. God's well of grace does NOT have a bottom to it. So, there is always grace to cover us (Romans 5:20). We do not have to feel guilty over something that God has already forgiven. We can let go of shame and take hold of grace.

> God is never shocked when we confess our sins. He is ready to forgive freely.

Dear fellow offspring of Adam and Eve, we never have to run and hide from Jesus when we have done something wrong. We can always come to him and tell him about our sins so we can receive mercy and forgiveness (Proverbs 28:13; Psalm 32:3-5). When we confess, God wipes our slate clean with love. He erases the list of offenses and never brings them up again or holds them against us (Psalm 103:2-

4,12). We can have joy knowing that because of his grace, love, and mercy we are forgiven, and God sees us just as if we had never sinned. Let us accept God's forgiveness and go forward, knowing that he will always love us as his very own.

We can let go of shame and take hold of grace.

And just know, God is not just interested in hearing our sins. He is a good, good father who wants to hear us confess our struggles, our true desires, and more. Though He knows them, He loves to talk with you and hear what is on your heart and mind.

Dear God, Thank you for being a God full of grace. Thank You for forgiving me, just as Your Word promised. Help me not to hide from You but come to You just as I am knowing that Your love for me is unconditional. I confess to You my sins and receive Your forgiveness. Amen.

Reflect: What regret, remorse, or guilt do you need release to God? Which of these verses will you memorize and meditate on to reassure you of God's grace and forgiveness: 1 John 1:9; Psalm 103:12; Proverbs 28:13; Psalm 32:3-5?

Joy of Obedience

Read: John 15:5-12

"When you obey my commandments, you remain in my love, just as I obey my Father's commandments and remain in His love. I have told you these things so that you will be filled with my joy. Yes, your joy will overflow!"
John 15:10-11 NLT

I love Taboo!! For those who have been totally missing out on life and do not know what Taboo is, let me explain. Taboo is a word guessing game. You have to get your teammates to say the 'Guess' word without saying the forbidden words. Now, imagine a Taboo card, with the guess word 'obedience' and 'joy' on the list of forbidden words.

> Jesus when talking to His disciples implied that the path to true joy is on the path of obedience to God (John 15:10-11).

Joy and obedience do not seem to fit together. Many of us probably view the two contradictorily. Joy seems liberating and conveys lightheartedness. When I think of joy, I think "oh yeah, fun!" Obedience sounds burdensome and conveys restrictions. When I think of obedience, I think "ugh, do I have to?" However, Jesus, when talking to His disciples [those who took up their cross, denied themselves, and willingly followed him], implied that the path to true joy is on the path of obedience to God (John 15:10-11). We can confidently obey him because he has our best interests at heart. As we obey, we "remain in his love" and are filled with joy (John 15:10-11). Obedience, from the heart to our gracious God, results in great joy.

I think one of the reasons we struggle to grasp the joy of obeying God is because we do not realize obedience to God opens avenues of blessing for us. When we voluntarily obey God, He gives us blessings beyond what we deserve (Deuteronomy 28:1-2). When we obey, God

Joyful Truth

When we voluntarily obey God, He gives us blessings beyond what we deserve (Deuteronomy 28:1-2). blesses us with long life, protection, and peace (Deuteronomy 5:33). Even more astounding is that when we are obedient, God blesses not only us but our descendants. Talk about an inheritance! (Genesis 22:18).

Jesus invites us to find joy in Him through our obedience. When done in love, obedience to God is not drudgery, it is joy. Our obedience, no matter how big or small, glorifies God. The more we choose to glorify God, the more joyful we will be. When we abide in Jesus and follow his commands, we have the promise of the fullness of joy.

Dear God, Lord, when you tell me to do something I will trust you and obey. Remind me that my obedience leads to blessings. Let me experience the joy and blessings of obeying you. Amen.

Reflect: What area of your life would be more joyful if you obeyed God? If you applied biblical principles? What would it be like to live with Jesus' complete joy in your heart?

_____

_____

_____

_____

_____

_____

_____

_____

_____

_____

_____

_____

_____

_____

_____

_____

_____

_____

_____

_____

_____

_____

_____

_____

_____

_____

_____

_____

_____

_____

_____

_____

Christmas Joy?

Read: Matthew 2:1-12

"But let all who passionately seek you erupt with excitement and joy over what you've done! Let all your lovers rejoice continually in the Savior, saying, "How great and glorious is our God!""
Psalm 40:16 TPT

Christmas, the most wonderful time of the year! Amid the many festivities, the holidays can be stressful for some. All the baking, cooking, decorating, shopping, partying, gifting, attending plays and concerts can sometimes overwhelm and exhaust even the most gleeful of souls. Some of us find ourselves longing for a little more of the joy Jesus came to bring into the world.

I am learning that if I want to avoid the stress of the season, I need to intentionally put Jesus on my to-do list. I must prioritize Him above all the things vying for my attention. I can gift myself with the freedom to say 'no.' It is okay for me (and you) to decline a few party invites, decide not to buy a few Christmas gifts, opt-out of another Christmas concert with a special rendition of Jingle Bells, and spend time with Jesus.

I suspect the wise men had to say 'no' too on their journey to worship Jesus. They traveled a great distance, approximately 1,000 miles from Egypt to Jerusalem, on horses. The journey would have occurred over several weeks (possibly months) meaning they would have stopped to rest, refresh, and relieve themselves. Nonetheless, the wise men did not get distracted on the way. They remained focused on their mission: to worship King Jesus.

As we seek Him, we'll discover the wonder, hope and joy found in Christ, that's available Christmas and year-round.

In the swirling busyness of December, it is a fight to keep Christ in Christmas, to keep Jesus at the center of it all. Many of us tend to overexert ourselves and spend too much time, money, and energy on things that drain us. However, we can enjoy the best Christmas has to offer, or really the best Jesus has to offer, by unplugging and spending time reconnecting with childlike awe at the wonder of Christmas.

Joyful Truth

Enjoy the best Jesus has to offer, by unplugging and spending time reconnecting with childlike awe at the wonder of Christmas.

Grab a cup of hot cocoa, apple cider, or eggnog ;-). Let us open our Bible and be reintroduced to Jesus: the reason for the season. Like the wise men, as we seek Him, we will discover the wonder, hope, and joy found in Christ; it is available on Christmas and year-round. We will celebrate and rejoice as we are reminded how Great our God is (Psalm 40:16). We will marvel at the salvation of the Father, given to us through His son Christ Jesus.

Dear God, I want to experience Your peace and joy this season. Speak to my heart and remind me to slow down and reflect on the true meaning of Christmas and the joy You bring to me. Thank You for Immanuel God with us. Amen.

Reflect: How can you declutter your life so you can meet with Jesus? List three things you will say no to or do to ensure you have time to experience Jesus' peace and joy.

_____
_____
_____
_____
_____
_____
_____
_____
_____
_____
_____
_____
_____
_____
_____
_____
_____
_____
_____
_____
_____
_____
_____
_____
_____
_____
_____
_____
_____
_____
_____
_____
_____
_____
_____
_____
_____
_____
_____

Joy in Liberty

Read: Galatians 5:1-10

"Let me be clear, the Anointed One has set us free—not partially, but completely and wonderfully free! We must always cherish this truth and stubbornly refuse to go back into the bondage of our past."
Galatians 5:1 TPT

One of my favorite group activities is an Escape Room. Working in a team of 4 or more, you find clues, solve puzzles, and try to escape a room in less than 60 minutes. Some of the clues and puzzles are super hard. Fortunately, you can reach out to the Game Master to offer you a clue (or simply let you out).

While overall it is a fun, exciting adventure, the reality is nobody likes being or feeling trapped. Fortunately, we have a Master who is also our Savior. Jesus came to set us free from any physical, mental, or emotional prison keeping us from becoming all he created us to be. We do not have to earn it or work for it. God willingly offers freedom to all who believe in him. We simply need to embrace and walk in freedom in Christ (Psalm 119:45).

> Jesus came to set us free from any physical, mental, or emotional prison keeping us from becoming all He created us to be.

In Christ, we are free from the bondage of sin, religious traditions, and perfectionism. Because of Christ's work on the cross, we are free to obey God out of love not out of a desire to earn a right standing with God. Freedom is God's goal for us, and he has given us the Holy Spirit to help us live in freedom. Knowing this, we should "cherish this truth and stubbornly refuse to go back into the bondage." We are free to find total and utter completion in Jesus and not a long list of man-made rules and expectations. We are free to follow Jesus out of love, not guilt, obligation, or coercion. We

Joyful Truth

We do not have to be guilt-driven into a life of religious performance. God calls us to live a love-driven life that flows from the heart.

can stand firm in Jesus' love and the power given to us through the finished work of Jesus on the cross.

We can experience the joy of freedom when we choose to live in light of what God has done through Jesus. We do not have to be guilt-driven into a life of religious performance. God calls us to live a love-driven life that flows from the heart. We have to let go of the burdens and chains. Every believer has been given the power to live free, we have to accept the gift. Joy and love await those who realize "if the Son sets you free, you will be free indeed" (John 8:36). Receive the gift of freedom that Jesus gave us through the cross.

Dear God, Thank you Christ Jesus for setting me free. Help me to live free and not get tangled up in situations that will put me back into the bondage from which You gave Your life to set me free. Help me to rest in the freedom of Christ and not be in bondage of any kind. Amen.

Reflect: How have you been kept from experiencing freedom in Christ? Pray and ask the Holy Spirit to reveal what actions you need to take toward freedom? (For example: pray for faith, choose forgiveness, focus on completion in Christ, etc.)

_____

_____

_____

_____

_____

_____

_____

_____

_____

_____

_____

_____

_____

_____

_____

_____

_____

_____

_____

_____

_____

_____

_____

_____

_____

_____

_____

_____

_____

_____

_____

_____

_____

Joy of Solitude

Read: Mark 1:32-39

"Very early in the morning, while it was still dark, Jesus got up, left the house, and went off to a solitary place, where he prayed."
Mark 1:35 NIV

We live in a culture where most of us are constantly connected and busy. The day starts with blaring alarms on our phones and notifications of what we have missed while sleeping. Our schedules are overfilled with meetings, activities, and to-dos. Our lives are packed full of more: doing more, achieving more, acquiring more leaving little time for peace and quiet.

We treat 'alone time' as an inconvenience, a punishment, a stigma. The truth is solitude is a blessing, not a burden. Solitude is an opportunity to sort through with the Father whatever is on our mind and in our heart. In solitude, we share with Him our fears, unfulfilled hopes, resentments, wounds, and worries. He lifts our burdens and gives us a new perspective. God is actively present in our lives—healing, teaching, and guiding. We need to set aside a time and space to reflect and acknowledge how He is moving in our lives.

> Solitude is a blessing, not a burden. Solitude is an opportunity to sort through with the Father whatever is on our mind and in our heart.

Jesus, God in the flesh, needed peace and quiet too. He needed solitude. People were always pulling and tugging at Him. There was always a need to be met; yet Jesus routinely withdrew to quiet places to be alone with God. Like Jesus, we need solitude. The daily cares of life take a toll on the body, mind, and soul. We need moments with just God where we intimately connect with Him and find our sufficiency and joy in him. We have to be intentional about withdrawing from our routines to a place of solitude. When we retreat to spend time with God our love-relationship with God grows and we get to know Him as Abba Father (Psalm 46:10).

Let us resist the rush. Let us halt the hustle. Let us break and breathe. Sit down and reflect with Jesus! Jesus was purposeful about His solitude. And we should be too. Let us continually withdraw from people and the demands of life to be alone with the Father and pray. When we step away from the crowd and draw near to God our body, mind, and soul are refreshed, strengthened, and renewed!

Joyful Truth

When we draw near to God our body, mind, and soul are refreshed, strengthened, and renewed!

Dear God, help me adopt a habit of rest and solitude. Give me the wisdom to carve out space and time to stop and be quiet with You. Let me experience the joy of being with You in quietness. Amen.

Reflect: Where in your schedule will you carve out solitude this week (even if just for 5 minutes)? What can you do during your times of solitude to truly recharge?

_____
_____
_____
_____
_____
_____
_____
_____
_____
_____
_____
_____
_____
_____
_____
_____
_____
_____
_____
_____
_____
_____
_____
_____
_____
_____
_____
_____
_____
_____
_____
_____
_____
_____

Joy of New

Read: Isaiah 43:16-21

"See, I am doing a new thing! Now it springs up; do you not perceive it? I am making a way in the wilderness and streams in the wasteland."
Isaiah 43:19 NIV

Have you ever noticed how excited people get over something new? New home, new clothes, new shoes, new friends. I have seen people receive used cars with the same excitement as someone receiving a new car. Why? Because even though it is a used car, it is new to them. Or how about someone with a new job? It could be the same position and function, but it is a new company, a new environment. While new can be daunting, new is often inspiring, exciting, and fun.

> Because of Jesus, we can daily experience the joy of the new. Jesus bore a cross so we could be made new and have a new perspective on life.

Because of Jesus, we can daily experience the joy of the new. Jesus bore a cross so we could be made new and have a new perspective on life. He sacrificed His life and conquered sin so we could be forgiven and can enjoy a new abundant life in Christ. We all sin and make mistakes. Fortunately, God's forgiveness enables us to start each morning with a clean slate. When we repent, He chooses to remember our sins no more (Hebrews 8:12). In Christ, we are new creations (2 Corinthians 5:17). And no, the newness is not instant, but gradual. (I, too, wish the transformation would snap like that.) As we follow Jesus' teachings and open our hearts and minds to his transforming power, our priorities, our values, our character, our perspectives, our attitudes, and our relationships become new over time.

Every day we are given new mercies, new grace (Lamentations 3:22-23). God's compassion and faithfulness are new every morning, so we can start afresh each day. God's mercy reaches beyond the muck and mire of our pasts to recreate us in the grace and love of Jesus. We can live beyond our disappointments, mistakes, and pains. In Isaiah 43:18-19, God encourages His people to let go of the old and embrace the new, even though this new seemed scary and unfamiliar.

Joyful Truth

Every day we are given new mercies, new grace (Lamentations 3:22-23).

Stop holding on to something God has already let go. Stop dragging old, dead things into the new, abundant life that Jesus' birth, death, and resurrection made possible. Stop mourning the past and start embracing the new with a heart full of faith and a mind full of optimism. When we embark on a new journey with Christ, let us walk with peace, hope, and joy. With Christ we can step into the new, no matter how scary and uncertain it may be, with courage, bravery, and an unsinkable faith.

Dear God, Thank You for this new day, Lord. Thank you for declaring me a new creation in Christ and doing a new and beautiful thing in my life. I am grateful that in Your kindness and mercy You have given me the promise of eternal life. Please change me from the inside out. Amen.

Reflect: How do you feel when God opens a new door for you? How can you make Isaiah 43:19 your prayer when entering a new season of life?

_____
_____
_____
_____
_____
_____
_____
_____
_____
_____
_____
_____
_____
_____
_____
_____
_____
_____
_____
_____
_____
_____
_____
_____
_____
_____
_____
_____
_____
_____
_____
_____
_____
_____
_____
_____
_____
_____
_____
_____

Joy of Trouble

Read: Romans 5:1-5

"But that's not all! Even in times of trouble we have a joyful confidence, knowing that our pressures will develop in us patient endurance."
Romans 5:3 TPT

To me, the apostle Paul is the uncle I love but can only take in doses because of his straight, "no filter" communication style. Paul's books in the New Testament are filled with a little conviction and a little love

to guide us on our spiritual walk and help us to better understand what it means to live out our faith. Often his words of wisdom are low-key cray, cray. Take this verse about suffering. Paul says, "rejoice in them...have joyful confidence." Wait, What?!? In times of trouble, trials, and tribulation I want to throw a major tantrum and cry (after I have done everything I can to get out of it quickly). How can Paul, tell us to rejoice, have joyful

> The key to having joyful confidence in times of trouble is what you know about who you know.

confidence, in our troubles?

In Romans 5:3, notice the word "knowing." That is the game-changer. Paul knows the key to having joyful confidence during trouble is what you know, moreover what you know about who you know. We know that God is good, faithful, and trustworthy. We know He is more than able to bring good out of the bad. In our troubles, we can have joyful confidence because we know our God is good, faithful, and trustworthy thus we can trust Him to develop perseverance, character, and hope within us (Romans 5:3-5). Our troubles are not catastrophes, but rather catalysts God uses to develop our character and strengthen our ability to trust Him at a deeper level through the challenges of life. He is at work in our struggles.

The goal is not to rejoice because of our difficult circumstances. But rather, to rejoice in knowing God is doing something amid our difficult circumstances. When disaster strikes, we tend to want God to immediately make everything better. But God gives us the faith to endure and tells us, "Don't give up. Grow up." God desires for us to learn to endure, to stick with it. He wants us to embrace his grace and strength as we go through difficulty without running away or looking for the easy way out. We are to look to Christ, His power, His sufficiency, His wisdom, and His love, and endure so we develop proven, firm, unbreakable faith.

Joyful Truth

Know God is doing something during your troubling circumstances.

To experience joy, we must trust our great Shepherd. We must trust and know He is with us through it all. God guides us and gives us indescribable joy, calming comfort, and overflowing peace during trouble. We can rejoice and exult in tribulation when we rest in the grace of God and trust in God's promises. He promised to be with us always, so you are not going through the trial alone (Matthew 28:20). Allow the joy of the Lord to be your strength and carry you through.

Dear God, Thank You for being with us in our trials, and for helping us to grow through them. Help me to remember that in good times or bad, You remain in control and have a plan for me. I thank You that I can rest in Your ever-abiding presence with me. Give me joy, peace, and the strength to keep going in the midst of the storm. Amen.

Reflect: How has God developed your character in times of trouble? What are some things you have learned about God and yourself while you were going through a time of trouble? How have those lessons helped you grow spiritually?

_____

_____

_____

_____

_____

_____

_____

_____

_____

_____

_____

_____

_____

_____

_____

_____

_____

_____

_____

_____

_____

_____

_____

_____

_____

_____

_____

_____

_____

_____

_____

_____

Joy of Sandpaper People

Read: Luke 6:27-36

"But I tell you who hear me: Love your enemies, do
good to those who hate you, bless those who curse
you, pray for those who mistreat you."
Luke 6:27-28 GNT

That coworker. That aunt. That cashier. That person driving too slow
in the fast lane. Most of us have that one person who for whatever
reason rubs us the wrong way and makes us use every bit of grace
and patience within us. These people are what I call sandpaper
people. (PS: Sandpaper people come in all shapes, sizes, and colors
and sometimes they are us!) Instead of magically making them go
away, God allows them in our lives so that he can smooth our rough
edges and develop our character for His purposes.

God puts everyone we encounter into our life for a reason. The
sandpaper people can be used by God to mold, reshape, and
sometimes stretch us as he perpetually crafts us into becoming more
and more like his Son. While we may want to knock them out, we
should be grateful for the sandpaper people. God does not want us to
change them, run from them, ignore them, and/or try to fix them.
Instead, he wants us to love them,
do good towards them, bless them
(speak well of them), and pray for
them.

Let us find joy in our interactions
with sandpaper people by seeing
them as a blessing. They are
helping us to grow emotionally and
spiritually. Sandpaper people are
'God-sent' teachers (not jerks)
helping to build our character and
make needed changes in our

> Sandpaper people can
> be used by God to
> stretch us as he
> perpetually crafts us into
> becoming more and
> more like His Son.

attitude and behavior. While they annoy, anger, frustrate, and test us,
God is using sandpaper people to bring out the best in us. Submit to
the smoothing process, rather than resist it. As we encounter difficult

Joyful Truth

As we love and treat people as Christ would, we will experience relationships at a whole new level.

people, by God's grace we can see and love them through His eyes. As we love and treat people as Christ would, we will experience relationships at a whole new level. And that can bring joy!

Dear God, Thank You for the sandpaper people. Help me to respond to them with love, grace, and patience as You do with me. Continue to mold me and smooth me so I may become more like You! Amen.

Reflect: Who are the difficult people in your life? How can responding to them in love and with prayer make a difference?

_____
_____
_____
_____
_____
_____
_____
_____
_____
_____
_____
_____
_____
_____
_____
_____
_____
_____
_____
_____
_____
_____
_____
_____
_____
_____
_____
_____
_____
_____
_____
_____
_____
_____

Joy of Hope

Read: Proverbs 10:25-30

"The hope of the righteous brings joy, but the expectation of the wicked will perish."
Proverbs 10:28 ESV

One trend that has emerged over the past decade or so is "gender reveal" parties. Gender reveals are filled with so much hope and anticipatory joy about the new life that is to come. Parents, friends, and family members are excited as they count down, then cut the cake or pop the balloon, revealing the gender of the promised, precious one.

It can be hard to have that same hope and anticipatory joy as we wait for God to reveal Himself in our situations. When days are dark and long, hope feels distant and elusive. As time passes, it becomes increasingly difficult to hope and trust God's heart, especially when we cannot see His hands. Yet on those days, hope and joy can seep in and permeate our hearts as we allow the Holy Spirit to speak to our hearts and remind us of God's hope, promised future, and power (Ephesians 1:18). When everything looks hopeless, true hope remains determined to believe in God's reality and His power to work all things together for our good(Romans 8:28)!

Walk closely with Him and lean on Him, being "joyful in hope, patient in affliction, faithful in prayer" (Romans 12:12).

As beloved of the everlasting God, we can have hope - a confident expectation - in the God who has spoken and revealed Himself and His limitless power in the Scriptures. Why? Because He took a tragic event and transformed it into a beautiful life-changing story. Yes, the Son of God, the savior of the world was murdered. But death was not the end of the story. God rolled the stone away and Jesus, hope personified, walked out of the grave. Let us hope in Jesus Christ, the author and perfecter our faith (Hebrews 12:2). He is still writing our story and the ending will not disappoint. Keeping our eyes on Jesus, the object of our hope and faith, will keep us from sinking under the weight of adversity, fuel our joy and help us endure.

Dear friend, when the diagnosis comes, the relationship struggles, the finances dry up, the dream is deferred, or whatever, let us stand firm in God and His Word. When circumstances are despairing and life is overwhelming, keep hoping and waiting on God (Psalm 42:5). Walk closely with Him and lean on Him, being "joyful in hope, patient in affliction, faithful in prayer" (Romans 12:12). Do not abandon hope but be filled with hope, joy, and peace as you wait in anticipation for God's promises to be fulfilled, with the greatest promise being Heaven (Romans 15:13). God will reveal Himself as a way-maker, promise keeper, deliverer, or whatever your situation requires.

Joyful Truth

Hope in Jesus Christ, the author and perfecter our faith (Hebrews 12:2). He is still writing our story and the ending will not disappoint.

Dear God, Thank You for hope that is strengthened through every trial. God help me have hope as I wait on You to show yourself faithful and good. Help me to remember that You may delay my request, but You will never disappoint my trust. May Your greatness and glory be evident in my life. Amen.

Reflect: What has disappointed you lately? How can you reach out for hope and trust that His promises will never disappoint?

_____

_____

_____

_____

_____

_____

_____

_____

_____

_____

_____

_____

_____

_____

_____

_____

_____

_____

_____

_____

_____

_____

_____

_____

_____

_____

_____

_____

_____

_____

_____

_____

_____

_____

_____

_____

_____

Joy of Not Being Afraid

Read: Luke 2:8-15

"But the angel reassured them. "Don't be afraid!" he said. "I bring you good news that will bring great joy to all people.""
Luke 2:10 NLT

Fear is a stubborn, persistent enemy of the human heart. Many of us battle it daily- fear of what people think, failing in life, disease, and death. Fear drains our energy and joy for life. But here's the good news: As followers of Christ, we do not have to be enslaved to fear. Fear does not have to control us or dictate our decisions.

In Luke 2, the shepherds (who were minding their business) were gripped by fear when not just one angel appeared, but a great many – an entire heavenly host! While fear seized them for a moment, the good news the angels shared freed them to continue in purpose.

When fear grips our heart, we must make a concerted effort to fight fear with God's word so we can experience the freedom and joy He freely gives.

"Fear not, I bring you good news." What was that good news? The good news is "the Savior has been born." The Savior is the one who will take away your fears. This is the Savior who is Immanuel, God with you(Matthew 1:22–23)!!

Fear is one of the enemy's most popular weapons. He uses fear to control our every move and decision. God knows we wrestle with fear so being the awesome defender who is mighty in battle (Psalm 24:8), He equipped us for our battle with fear long before we were even born. We can fight fear by daily putting our trust in God and His word.There are numerous Bible verses that tell us not to be afraid. When fear grips our heart, we must make a concerted effort to fight fear with God's word so we can experience the freedom and joy He freely gives.

Joyful Truth

God is always with you (Deuteronomy 31:8). Ditch fear, get moving, and do the great things God has planned for you.

What would your life be like if fear didn't hold you back? Would your mundane life be interrupted with great purpose and astonishment as you, like the shepherds, brought great joy to people by spreading the Good News? Do not allow fear to control you, hold you back, or paralyze you in its grasp. Do not allow fear to cause you to buckle and settle for less than God's best. Push past the fears into joy, knowing God is always with you (Deuteronomy 31:8, Matthew 28:20). Ditch fear, get moving, and do the great things God has planned for you. You do not have to bury your dreams in shallow graves of fear, but live in bold obedience expecting the best.

Dear God, Thank you for not giving us a spirit of fear, but of power, love, and self-control. God ease my fears and calm my heart. Help me to remember that I don't have to be afraid of any challenge I'm facing because You're with me. I know that You are faithful, loving, and kind. Help me to trust in Your Sovereignty, knowing that You are in control. Build my faith and help me to rely on Your presence and support no matter what I face. Amen.

Reflect: Are there situations in life causing you to be afraid? What Scripture(s) can you remember and meditate on to help you combat fear? Place the Scripture(s) somewhere easily visible to remind you to not be afraid.

_____
_____
_____
_____
_____
_____
_____
_____
_____
_____
_____
_____
_____
_____
_____
_____
_____
_____
_____
_____
_____
_____
_____
_____
_____
_____
_____
_____
_____
_____
_____
_____
_____
_____
_____

Joy of His Presence

Read: Psalm 16:7-11

"You make known to me the path of life; you will fill me with joy in your presence, with eternal pleasures at your right hand."
Psalm 16:11 NIV

Have you ever asked yourself "how did my life turn out this way?" I remember trying to figure out that question my senior year of college when it became clear to me that I was not going to medical school after graduation. All of the plans I made for myself seemed so out of reach. I was on a new path and really needed God to give me a glimpse of what lay ahead and hope that my life was not going to be a failure. I imagine David might have felt this way. The celebrated hero who defeated Goliath and had been anointed the next king of Israel was now on the run from King Saul, his best friend's dad (1 Samuel 21)!

> God's path doesn't mean a life without trouble. Amidst the difficult circumstances, we can experience joy in the presence of the Savior who is near!

In Psalm 16, David makes it clear that following God's path does not mean a life without trouble. Amidst the difficult circumstances, David realized he could look to God and find the joy that supersedes circumstances. Even at his lowest, David could still praise God and experience the joy of being in His presence because he understood that real joy comes from trusting God and His faithfulness. When our plans seem to be falling apart, we, too, can trust and look to God for refuge, rest, peace, and wisdom. God is near; He will not abandon us, even in death (Romans 8:38). We can experience joy in the presence of the Savior who is near!

A life of joy is found in keeping company with Jesus, not a life void of difficulty. When the going gets tough do not get lost in the depths of sadness and heartbreak, rather get into the presence of God. We can daily

Keep walking with God on His path for you and stay in His presence the only place where there is "fullness of joy" and "pleasures forever".

experience his presence and the fullness of joy through prayer and time in his word. When we pray, we acknowledge that God is present with us and there is no such thing as impossible. When we read the Bible, we are encountering the presence of God in a unique, powerful way. In other words, have a spiritual conversation with God who both hears and answers us.

Keep walking with God on his path for you and stay in his presence the only place where there is "fullness of joy" and "pleasures forever." The more we choose to come near, affirming our trust in him, the more we can learn to be joyful in hope while waiting in his presence—where joy abounds.

Dear God, Thank you God for the fullness of joy that can only be found in Your presence. Thank you for being my guide. Help me to draw close to you and experience this joy as I walk with You. I want to find joy in the life You have planned for me. Amen.

Reflect: Look at your calendar this week. When can you schedule at least 15 minutes to sit at Jesus' feet and read Psalm 84? When you read Psalm 84, write what stands out to you about the presence of God?

_____
_____
_____
_____
_____
_____
_____
_____
_____
_____
_____
_____
_____
_____
_____
_____
_____
_____
_____
_____
_____
_____
_____
_____
_____
_____
_____
_____
_____
_____
_____
_____
_____

Joy of Justice

Read: Proverbs 21:10-21

"When justice is done, it brings joy to the righteous but terror to evildoers."
Proverbs 21:15 ESV

Our world is full of injustices. Human trafficking. Child abuse. Elder abuse. The killing of innocent lives without repercussions. As we listen to these stories on the news or read headlines on Twitter, within many of us our innate sense of right and wrong begins to rise like lava in a volcano. Having been made in his image (Genesis 1:26-27), we naturally long for justice to prevail upon the earth and are outraged when we see injustice happening around us. It can be easy to constantly feel despair. We wonder where God is in the midst of these injustices, wondering if he even cares. God is here and he most certainly cares (1 Peter 5:7, Psalm 55:22). He cares more about righting wrongs than we ever could, and he will bring justice.

> Jesus demonstrates that bringing justice to earth is going to take more than an occasional prayer; bringing justice requires sincere action from those who claim to be His children.

God is a just God. Justice is one of God's attributes. It flows out of his holiness. As followers of Christ, justice should be a trait that defines us (Micah 6:8; Luke 11:42). God is concerned about justice from the womb to the tomb (and we should be too). Jesus demonstrates a beautiful example for us to follow. Remember when he scolded the disciples for turning away the children (Matthew 19:13-14)? Or when he touched and healed the leper (Mark 1:40-45)? Or when he fed the over 5,000 hungry men, women, and children rather than telling them to go find food on their own (Matthew 14:13-21)? Or when he healed and spoke to the woman with the issue of blood (Luke 8:43–48)? In these moments, Jesus demonstrates that bringing justice to earth is going to take more than an occasional prayer; bringing justice requires sincere action from those who claim to be his children.

God invites us to experience the joy of justice and be part of setting things right. He invites us to be a visible expression of His love and care. Inaction against injustice is not a Biblical option. We, as Christians, have to stand up for those who are experiencing oppression and injustice (Proverbs 31:8-9). If we are to love as God loves us, we need to stand for change. We have to change how we treat others, how we support others, and how we view others. While change may

> ### Joyful Truth
>
> God is a just God. God invites us to experience the joy of justice and be part of setting things right. He invites us to be a visible expression of His love and care.

be uncomfortable, we cannot allow discomfort and fear to silence the need to stand with those being treated as less than because of their race, national origin, sex, sexual orientation, gender identity, religion, or disability status. God's word tells us to move past our affiliations, comfort zones, and do what each of us can to be an advocate for those we come across who need our help being heard and who do not have access to the justice they deserve.

To act justly, love mercy, and walk humbly with God is no easy task, but it is a worthy calling. It starts by seeing people as God sees them – recognizing that we are all created in the image of God. Upholding justice consists of a broad range of activities, from fair and honest dealings with people in daily life, to generously giving your time and resources to activism that seeks to end particular forms of injustice, violence, and oppression. As we apply God's heart of justice, we will see ourselves and others changed as the kingdom of heaven comes to earth. As 2 Peter 3:13 says, we are promised that someday, when Christ physically reigns on earth, God's righteous justice will finally be on full display.

Dear God, Thank you for being our God of justice, mercy, and truth (Ps. 89:14). Help us to adopt your sense of justice. Use me to speak up for those who cannot speak for themselves. Guide me as I aim to live with compassion, love, and seek justice for those in need. May our hearts fill with joy, as we daily do what is right and just, and wait for You to bring total justice. Amen.

Reflect: Why do you think it's so important for Christians to stand up for justice? What can you do to promote justice more faithfully?

Joy of Faithfulness

Read: Luke 16:1-12

"One who is faithful in a very little is also faithful in much, and one who is dishonest in a very little is also dishonest in much."
Luke 16:10 ESV

Am I the only one that is quick to think that quitting is an option when the journey gets rough, murky, and more than you signed up before? No? Great! We can continue.

In 2015, I started recording daily sermonettes. On social media, I would share a lesson God taught me. I was often disappointed when I would see less than 50 likes or views. However, I still delivered each sermonette with passion as if I had thousands of viewers. Fast forward to 2018, when my church asked me to give the welcome during the service, which included giving short sermonettes to thousands of attendees. When reflecting and praying about it, God reminded me that faithfulness matters. Whether I had an audience of 5, 50, or 50,000, I needed to be obedient and faithful. I am called to be faithful, not famous. I, you, we must be faithful to what God has called us to do knowing that the only reward may be "Well done, my good and faithful servant."

Our faithfulness to follow him in small steps demonstrates we can be trusted to follow him in big steps. The principle of being faithful in little so that we may later be entrusted with more applies to our finances, relationships, integrity, talents/skills, and service to God. The joy of faithfulness comes not only when God gives us greater things (i.e. more resources, greater opportunities, or increased

The joy of faithfulness comes not only when God gives us greater things but also when we see how our faithfulness and the greater things draw more people to God.

Joyful Truth

There is joy to be found in living a life of faithfulness and service to Jesus!! Stay the path.

influence) but also when we see how our faithfulness and the greater things draw more people to God and bless others.

While it can be extremely difficult at times, we must be faithful to assignments God has given us. No matter how big and extravagant the dreams God has placed on our hearts are, the journey to those dreams begins with being obedient in the small things first. It is in going about our daily lives with faithfulness, honesty, and humility that God often reveals to us His larger plan. God rewards and expands our territory when we demonstrate our faithfulness in small things. Even when it is uncomfortable, hurtful, and confusing we cannot quit doing what He has called us to do.

Listen friend, there is joy to be found in living a life of faithfulness and service to Jesus!! Stay the path. God sees what we are going through. Moreover, He knows where He is taking us. And He says that if we are faithful in little things, He will give us greater and greater responsibility.

Dear God, I choose to be faithful. I want to be someone You can count on and someone others can count on. Help me to experience Your joy as I serve you faithfully, even in tough times. I want to make the best use of the abilities, spiritual gifts, and opportunities which You have entrusted to me. Amen.

Reflect: What would it look like to be faithful, if God said you would never be famous? What are the small things God has entrusted to you? How have you shown faithfulness in the care of those things?

_____
_____
_____
_____
_____
_____
_____
_____
_____
_____
_____
_____
_____
_____
_____
_____
_____
_____
_____
_____
_____
_____
_____
_____
_____
_____
_____
_____
_____
_____
_____
_____
_____
_____
_____
_____
_____

Joy of Rejection

Read: Psalm 118:19-29

"The stone which the builders rejected has become the chief cornerstone." Psalm 118:22 NKJV

"We've chosen another candidate," I read that phrase so many times in the months leading up to and following my college graduation. I applied to numerous jobs, would hope, pray, and wait...then receive a 'no.' I was down and wondering if God had forsaken me. It was not until months into my first job that I realized why God had allowed me to be rejected. God was not overlooking me; he was positioning me. In my first job, I met my prayer partner for the past five years and brought a colleague to church.

We have all been painfully rejected at one time or another. Whether it was not making the team, not being asked out on a date, not getting the job, or not being invited to the gathering. It does not matter how big or small, rejection hurts and sucks! Rejection often marks our hearts with pain and fear, then it leaves us questioning our sense of worth and belonging. We may even begin to wonder if God truly created us with purpose.

Rejection at times is God ordained. God will close doors to get us where he needs us to be. He is not overlooking; He is positioning.

Our rejections put us in good company. Jesus was rejected. Joseph was rejected. David was rejected. Not only were they rejected, but they were rejected by those closest to them. They were seen as less than, though they were royalty. After many trials and much time, God allowed each to be seen as the valiant leader they were all along. Though it often hurts, rejection is not always a bad thing. Rejection, in fact, at times is God ordained. In his mercy, God allows us to be rejected to protect and direct us. God will close doors, shut windows, block roads to get us where he needs us to be.

Rejection can be a defining moment, but it is not what defines us. God has already defined us.

Find joy in knowing that God still works all things for good, even rejection. Rejection can be a springboard launching us into a new season of purpose. We are not being pushed aside; we are being set apart. We are not being pushed back; we are being called forth. Rejection can be a defining moment, but it is not what defines us. God has already defined us. He says we are accepted, chosen, and loved unconditionally and eternally. No rejection changes that.

Dear God, I am grateful that even when I feel overlooked, I can rest in the fact that I am handpicked by you. Change my perspective and help me to see you at work in all things. When I am rejected by people, help me to remember that I am loved by you. Amen.

Reflect: Is there a situation in your life that has made you feel rejected, left out, overlooked, or less than? When you feel this way speak these words out loud: "I am handpicked and called by God. I may be rejected by others, but I am forever cherished and accepted by the Most High God!"

Joy of Praise and Worship

Read: Psalm 95:1-10

"Come on, everyone! Let's sing for joy to the Lord! Let's shout our loudest praises to our God who saved us!"
Psalm 95:1 TPT

More than singing a few songs, more than a 15-minute agenda item on a church program, praise and worship (P&W) is an outward expression of our gratitude to our Lord God. P&W is more than

emotions. It is an outpouring of our admiration of God. We should praise God because of the spectacular works he has done and because of who He is. He is the God of peace, hope, wisdom, power, and much more!!

> Whatever struggle we are facing worship strengthens us for the fight and has the power to alter the course of the battle.

So where does the joy come in with praise and worship? The joy comes with the blessings of praise and worship. When we praise and worship God, we receive the blessing of peace in our own hearts and lives. While praise and worship is NOT a shortcut to receiving blessings from God, it does come with blessings. When we develop a lifestyle of praise and worship, we are blessed with a closer relationship with God, stronger faith, clarity and direction, and encouragement.

The joy also flows from the transforming power of P&W. P&W does not magically change our situations. It changes our perspectives. P&W shifts our focus away from the circumstances of life and toward the character of God. As we worship, we experience joyful, heartfelt, hope-filled delight in the God of mercy and grace. We enter into His presence and are reminded of His presences, the joy of His infinite love, and His power to do exceedingly and abundantly above all we ask or think. As we worship, we grasp God's greatness and ascribe to Him all the honor that is due to Him. Our faith is strengthened. Our hearts are encouraged. Our vision of God grows.

In Psalm 95, we are invited to lift our voice to proclaim the character and greatness of God. We are invited to make a joyful noise (the way we would at a sports game or concert). Dear fellow worshipper lift up your voice. Not sure what to say? A simple, yet powerful way to worship is to say, "Thank You, God, for being who You are." Then think about who He is: provider, savior, protector, healer, friend... to name a few. Whatever struggle we are facing worship strengthens us for the fight and has the power to alter the course of the battle. Let us join the great chorus of creation praising Him without ceasing.

Joyful Truth

Praise and Worship shifts our focus ... toward the character of God.

Dear God, Thank You for just being You! You are more awesome than I know. Thank You for everything that makes You magnificent. I stand in awe of You as I praise You with word and song. Amen.

Reflect: What prompts you to praise God? What songs help you to remember and focus on His character and goodness?

Joy of Brokenness

Read: Psalm 34:15-22

"The Lord is near to the brokenhearted and saves the crushed in spirit."
Psalm 34:18 NIV

I tried to be careful. I really did. But somehow the vase slipped out of my hand, crashed to the floor, and exploded into pieces. It was beyond repair. Have you had a similar experience? Perhaps it was a mug, a piece of china, or even your life. In one way or another, most, if not all of us, are familiar with broken things.

When we are broken, suffering, and in pain, it is tempting to believe God has abandoned us. We may think that God is a million miles away, but God draws us closer to Himself in the midst of our brokenness. God remains with those who are broken and makes them stronger than before (Psalm 147:2-3). God comes to the mess, gathers the broken pieces, and repairs and creates. Moreover, He heals our brokenness. We do not have to be ashamed of the lines that show we are broken vessels. They have an amazing story to tell. They are reminders of God holding us together with peace, hope, love, compassion, and joy.

Our brokenness leads us to a place where we are better able to see God and His power at work within our lives (Matthew 5:3). Brokenness can leave us feeling discouraged, unhappy, crushed, and bitter. Time alone will not heal our deep wounds; however, time, God's truth, and His healing power can transform our wounds into something wonderful, our bruises into something beautiful. Like a stained-glass window, in our brokenness, the light of Christ dazzles–drawing attention to His beauty; and making our lives beautiful as a result. He is the master at

> Like a stained-glass window, in our brokenness, the light of Christ dazzles–drawing attention to His beauty and making our lives beautiful as a result.

manufacturing amazing "stained glass windows"—pieces of broken glass that, on their own, look like disasters, but when grouped together by a skillful artist, create something uniquely beautiful. When the season of brokenness passes, you and others will marvel at the greatness of God.

Joyful Truth

Be encouraged, be joyful. God makes beautiful things out of broken things.

Be encouraged, be joyful. God makes beautiful things out of broken things. No matter how broken we may think we are, we are never too shattered for repair. God mends our brokenness with love, grace, mercy, and hope and brings forth new beauty, strength, and inspiration.

Dear God, Thank You for being near me in my brokenness. Thank you for healing the brokenhearted. May I experience Your very real presence. Use Your timeless truths to bind my wounds and make me whole. Amen.

Reflect: When have you felt broken or bruised? How did you experience God's presence? Ask God to use your broken pieces for your good and His glory.

_____

_____

_____

_____

_____

_____

_____

_____

_____

_____

_____

_____

_____

_____

_____

_____

_____

_____

_____

_____

_____

_____

_____

_____

_____

_____

_____

_____

_____

_____

Joy of Humility

Read: James 4:6-10

"He mocks proud mockers but shows favor to the
humble and oppressed."
Proverbs 3:34 NIV

Long before Kendrick Lamar told us to 'Be Humble, Sit Down'...God did. Though choosing to be humble is difficult, choosing to be humble comes with blessings. In choosing humility, we unleash more opportunities to experience grace. The more we receive God's grace, the less likely we are to exhaust ourselves trying to do everything in our own strength and ability.

We need to be humble and sit down at the feet of Jesus. Lay down our pride and surrender to God and His plan for our lives. When we are prideful we can be weighed down and overburden by fears, struggles, and heartaches ignoring the blessed truth that we have a heavenly Father who is capable of handling the cares that overwhelm us and is ready to lift our burdens (1 Peter 5:6-7). When we are

humble, we are more mindful of His sovereignty in our daily lives and the reality that as humans we have limitations while He is limitless. Humility acknowledges our desperate need for God. Laying down pride leads to a life that is richer, freer, and more abundant.

> Humility does not mean thinking of yourself less. It is thinking of God more, acknowledging His divine hand, and depending on His all-sufficient grace.

We can be humble and give our cares to God. Humility does not mean thinking of yourself less. It is thinking of God more, acknowledging His divine hand, and depending on His all-sufficient grace. Humility is choosing to acknowledge the mighty sovereign power of God. When we are humble, we are freeing ourselves from the overwhelming thoughts of how we must constantly strive and earn. When we operate in pride, we are constantly trying to prove, "I am fully capable of handling whatever life throws at me." When we walk in humility, we declare, "I have an almighty, all-powerful, limitless Father who empowers me to do what He has called me to do." When we are humble and admit that we cannot make it through a situation on our own, God opens the floodgates of heaven and pours out His grace.

> **Joyful Truth**
>
> We can experience the joy of humility as we place our confidence in God and His abilities.

God is not opposed to greatness. God is opposed to pride. Big difference. There is nothing wrong with receiving accolades for accomplishments and success; however, we must not forget to acknowledge the One who calls us. Pride leads to anxiety, sin, and even death. Humility leads to God's favor and protection. When we humble ourselves, God will lift us up as He sees fit (and when He sees fit) to elevate Himself (Luke 14:11).

Choose humility and experience the joy of thinking more about the greatness of God. We can experience the joy of humility as we place our confidence in God and his abilities, instead of being limited by a blind belief in our own abilities or disabilities.

Dear God, Thank You for the grace You bring to us through humility. Search my heart for any shred of pride and remove it. Help me live a life of humble and complete, total surrender to You. Please refine me to think, respond, and live humbly. Let my life be an arrow that points to Your greatness. Thank you for your grace that enables me to be humble. Amen.

Reflect: In what ways do you try to be self-sufficient? How does humbling yourself and relying on God more allow you to experience grace and joy?

_____

_____

_____

_____

_____

_____

_____

_____

_____

_____

_____

_____

_____

_____

_____

_____

_____

_____

_____

_____

_____

_____

_____

_____

_____

_____

_____

_____

_____

Joy of God's Discipline

Read: Psalm 30:1-12

"For his anger lasts only a moment, but his favor lasts a lifetime; weeping may stay for the night, but rejoicing comes in the morning."
Psalm 30:5 NIV

When we read some of the stories in the Old Testament, it is easy to envision God as this vengeful and mean being. This is why I think it is essential to read the Bible in context in order to get the facts. Look at the story of Uzzah, found in 1 Chronicles 13:9-12.

David desired to bring the ark of God back to Jerusalem. As the ark was being transported, the oxen pulling the cart stumbled, and a man named Uzzah took hold of the ark. God struck Uzzah down and he died. Now, I know you are probably thinking, "Whoa! That's nuts! God struck old dude dead because he touched the ark?!?! That's drastic." Let's go back to the book of Exodus to learn why God took such severe action.

God is for us (and NOT against us) He cannot stand by and watch us head down the wrong path.

God had given Moses and Aaron specific instructions about the movement of the Ark of the Covenant (Numbers 4:15; Exodus 25:12-14; Numbers 7:9). Uzzah was of a Levitical family and knew how the Ark was to be transported (Deuteronomy 31:9). Israel had previously carried the Ark of the Covenant in the right way (Joshua 3). Uzzah, David, and Israel knew what would happen if God's instructions were not followed. David deviated from those instructions and had begun to mess around with God's holiness. His disobedience and neglect of God's holiness, as does ours, came with a price. David realized the error of his ways.

David penned Psalm 30 after his second attempt to move the ark was successful. When David reflected on all the events leading up to the successful move of the ark, he realized that the death of Uzzah, though devastating and shocking, was a chastening act of love. The Lord was setting David and the children of Israel back on the path from which they were straying. Yes, night comes, but so does the morning. Weeping comes, but so does joy. God disciplined them for their disobedience, but He also favored them. See, favor is God's "I am for you" attitude. Since God is for us (and NOT against us), he cannot stand by and watch us head down the wrong path. God's discipline is never meant to hurt us; it is meant to redeem and restore us.

> ### Joyful Truth
>
> God's discipline is meant to redeem and restore us. When God disciplines us, He is not getting us back; He is drawing us back.

Sometimes the difficulty and pain we experience is a product of our sinful actions, careless attitude, or indifference towards God or others. God's discipline is not the sentence for our sin. The punishment for our sin was laid on Jesus at the cross, once and forever. Hardship and suffering are not God's way of getting even. Neither is it His means of retaliating for the wrongs we have committed. God disciplines us so we might become more and more like His Son, Jesus Christ.

When God disciplines us, He is not getting us back; He is drawing us back. He seeks to bring us back to His will and away from that which will destroy us. God's discipline flows out of His love for us. God's love confronts and corrects sin. God is a good, good Father who will correct us because He loves us (Hebrews 12:11). He wants to bless, help, and promote us. We are His children. When on the receiving end of discipline, we hate it. We cry and groan. Know this though: God promises to bring forth fruit from discipline such as peace, wholeness, and joy.

Dear God, I am grateful Your favor outlasts Your anger. Thank You for loving me enough to guide me to truth and steer me away from sin and error. Thank You for Your chastening love. I open my heart to Your correction. Father, whatever it takes, make me more like You. Bring forth a harvest of righteousness and peace in my life. Amen.

Reflect: How does it make you feel to know that God's discipline flows out of His love for you? What is one way you can be more open and responsive to God's correction in your life?

Joy of Contentment

Read: 1 Timothy 6:3-10

"Actually, godliness is a great source of profit when it is combined with being happy with what you already have."
1 Timothy 6:6 CEB

I loved my brand-new Toyota RAV 4 I was happy with my car, until three months later I saw the new model of the Toyota RAV 4. My shiny new car now seemed old and inadequate. When the mailing from the dealer came feeding my desire for an upgrade, I honestly contemplated trading in my car for a newer version. As I thought about it, I remembered that buying a new car would not make me content. It may result in temporary joy, but the happiness would only last until the next new model was released. I needed to be content and grateful.

We will always battle with discontentment until we let Christ be all that we need. He alone can bring us the peace and contentment we will never find in the pursuits of this life. How do we do this? We must choose to be thankful and focused on God's goodness to us. The Godliness that reaps contentment is a God-centered life. Contentment comes from having the right priority--godliness, not gain; and the right perspective—the eternal, not the temporal. Godly contentment trusts that God will provide what we need when we need it (Philippians 4:19).

> Contentment comes from having the right priority--godliness, not gain; and the right perspective—the eternal, not the temporal.

Paul says in Philippians 4:11, "I have learned to be content whatever the circumstances." Notice the word "learned." Contentment does not come naturally or instantaneously. For most of us, it is easier to grumble, complain, and focus on all that is missing rather than to be thankful for all we have. Contentment is a discipline developed over time as we practice gratitude; stop comparing ourselves to others; and stop searching for happiness in material things. Through the schoolhouse of life, God matures to the point that our contentment is not found in possessions, but in Christ.

If we want to experience greater joy, we must learn to be content with what God has given us and not feel like we must acquire more. The pursuit of happiness in material things often leads to disappointment and loss (money, relationships, time, character, and more). We have to cultivate an attitude that is grateful for what we have and moreover recognizes that God is enough. Quick side note: Contentment is not equivalent to complacency. We are to pursue greater heights, directed by God not our selfish ambitions. Continue to learn, grow, and discover. Amid success and prosperity, keep God as the priority.

Dear God, I trust that You are enough and You are good. You are my sufficiency. You are the greatest blessing of my life! Help me to live contentedly with all that You are today. Help me refocus my heart and find contentment right here, in this place You so graciously provided for me. Amen.

Reflect: What areas of your life are you least content? Learning to be contentment is a process. What is one step you can take today to be practice contentment?

_____

_____

_____

_____

_____

_____

_____

_____

_____

_____

_____

_____

_____

_____

_____

_____

_____

_____

_____

_____

_____

_____

_____

_____

_____

_____

_____

_____

_____

_____

_____

Joy in the Midst of Grief

Read: John 16:16-24

"So for now you are in grief, but I will see you again, and [then] your hearts will rejoice, and no one will take away from you your [great] joy."
John 16:22 AMP

Let's make this very clear. It is okay, acceptable, normal, Godly, and healthy to grieve. I am not sure when or how in Christendom we made grieving something that faithless people do. Somehow, we twisted 1 Thessalonians 4:13-18 and think because we know someone is 'in heaven, no longer suffering, or in a better place' that we should not drop any tears. WHAT?!?!? Jesus knew he was going to resurrect after three days and yet never belittles the grief his disciples would feel when he was being tortured and murdered (John 16:20-22). God is not disappointed or mad when we grieve. God created our emotions, and it is acceptable to grieve when sorrow comes to us along the road of life. He knows that to truly experience healing after grief, we must acknowledge the hurt of grief.

> God created our emotions and it is acceptable to grieve when sorrow comes to us along the road of life.

Grief is not an easy or straightforward process. Alongside grief, we experience a myriad of emotions including joy. Yes, it is possible for us to carry grief and joy together. How? First, we have to be honest about our emotions. We come just as we are to the One who knows us completely and loves us faithfully. We bring our honest grief to God. We do not need to hide our emotions. As we pour out and express our emotions, we make room for joy, hope, and peace. Second, we dig into God's word. God's word can bring hope to what seems hopeless with its wonderful promises and reminders of His caring and comforting presence (Psalm 119:50). God's living and active word has truths to heal our gaping wounds and gives us joy in the midst of grief as we trust Him for the future. Third, and perhaps most importantly, we remember

Joyful Truth

When we grieve, God does not abandon us and leave us grief-stricken. Rather, He draws nearer and remains with us as we journey toward healing and recovery.

God is near during painful times. God surrounds us with His peaceful, loving, and comforting presence (Psalm 119:76). We have His promise that we are never alone (Matthew 28:20; Hebrews 13:5). Though we may feel alone, He is with us right here, right now, always and forever. When we grieve, God does not abandon and leave us grief-stricken. Rather, He draws nearer and remains with us as we journey through confusion, anger, and sadness toward healing and recovery.

Dear fellow disciple, we have a Savior who does not merely know about our pain; He lived it. He knows and cares. We can confidently invite the One who endured the ultimate suffering into ours. As we take the time to process through our grief, let us invite Christ into it. No matter how long the grieving process, God wants to be with us through it. Ask Him to help you experience him in the midst of your grief.

Grief, loss, and pain are an inevitable scary and messy part of life. Facing the death of someone you love—a child, a spouse, a parent, a close friend—is one of life's most difficult experiences. God is with us as our comforter as we navigate through loss and death (Isaiah 66:13). God mercifully reaches down to comfort us and meet us where we are. One day our grief will be turned into joy. Until then, let us cling to his promises and allow ourselves to process emotions such as frustration, pain, shock, and grief. Let us put our cares into His hands and make room for His peace and hope in our hearts

Dear God, loss hurts. It is frustrating and difficult to accept that life can never be the same again. But I thank You for Your promises that bring hope and comfort. See me through this painful experience with Your grace. Amen.

Reflect: What are some misconceptions in our society that keep us from being comfortable with sharing our grief with God? If you are grieving, what are some ways you can release your grief so God can begin to heal your heart (i.e. journaling, prayer, talking to someone, crying)?

_____
_____
_____
_____
_____
_____
_____
_____
_____
_____
_____
_____
_____
_____
_____
_____
_____
_____
_____
_____
_____
_____
_____
_____
_____
_____
_____
_____
_____
_____
_____

Joy of Kindness

Read: 2 Samuel 9:1-13

"One day David asked, "Is anyone in Saul's family still alive—anyone to whom I can show kindness for Jonathan's sake?""
2 Samuel 9:1 NLT

My man David! I love that dude. He is one of the most complex, interesting Bible characters. If you do not know David, let me get you hip to some headlines from his life:

"Back then they didn't want me, now I'm hot they all on me: Young Shepherd boy defeats Giant and Gains major fan club"

"On the Run Tour Part I: Future King Runs for Life, Hunted by Best Friend's Father"

"TMZ Exclusive: King David's Affair with Bathsheba and His Attempts to Cover it Up"

Amid these headlines, there is a quieter story that does not scream so loudly for our attention; yet has powerful application to us all. It is the story of Mephibosheth (2 Samuel 9).

In times when it is hard to be kind, let Jesus be the example and inspiration.

Mephibosheth was the son of Jonathan (David's best friend) and grandson of King Saul (David's worst enemy). Because of the wickedness of King Saul, David could have seen Mephibosheth as a threat and had him killed. David could have chosen to bring 'closure' to a painful and traumatic period in his life by hurting and punishing Mephibosheth for the wrongs of his grandfather. However, David chose to move past his hurts and chose integrity and kindness.

David intentionally showed the steadfast love of the Lord to Mephibosheth, going against the norm. In those days, typically the king of a new dynasty killed anyone connected with the prior dynasty. But not David. David went against the principle of revenge and self-preservation. He did not allow the pain and trauma from Saul's wicked actions to keep him from honoring an oath he made to Jonathan (1 Samuel 20:15-16, 42). He found and showed kindness to Mephibosheth.

Fellow chosen ones, let us clothe ourselves with kindness and go against the norm (Colossians 3:12; 2 Corinthians 6:6). Though it may not always feel good to be kind, especially when it is toward someone who has not been kind to us, it is necessary in order to free us. For those of us struggling with bitterness and revenge, perhaps the key is kindness. In times when it is hard to be kind, let Jesus be the example and inspiration. While hanging on a cross, he looked with love and compassion on the people who crucified him and said, "Father, forgive them" (Luke 23:34). That truth is mind-blowing to me! Jesus, through the Holy Spirit, can help us be kind, even when it is not easy. When we choose kindness over bitterness, we gain freedom, peace, and joy.

Joyful Truth

Let us clothe ourselves with kindness. When we choose kindness over bitterness, we gain freedom, peace, and joy.

Dear God, May my life be marked by kindness so that others will see You in me. Motivate me to show someone else the same kindness You have shown me. Amen.

Reflect: Who can you show God's kindness to? What specific act of kindness can you demonstrate to someone who is hurting or discouraged?

_____

_____

_____

_____

_____

_____

_____

_____

_____

_____

_____

_____

_____

_____

_____

_____

_____

_____

_____

_____

_____

_____

_____

_____

_____

_____

_____

_____

_____

Joy of Waiting

Read: Psalm 33:16-22

"We wait for the Lord. He is our help and our shield. In him our hearts find joy. In His holy name we trust."
Psalm 33:20-21 GW

Let's pretend we are all in a room. If we were to go around the room right now, I guarantee that each of us could tell a story about something we are waiting on God to change, to act, to move, to deliver, or to rescue. While we wait, we wonder, "Why does God make us wait? Why can't God ascribe to the J.G. Wentworth way of life and give me what is mine now?"

It is so excruciatingly hard to wait on the Lord as we dwell in the space between prayer offered and prayer answered. Here, there is a war between fact and feeling, between what we know to be true and the emotions we are experiencing. We know God will never abandon us, but we feel forgotten, alone, and distant from the One who answers our prayers (1 John 5:14-15, Psalm 40:1). So how do we have joy while we wait? How do we wait for God to bring a spouse? To give life to a barren womb? To save a wandering child? To repair a once-treasured, now shattered relationship? To provide the resources to start the business? To allow us to be recognized for our work and promoted? We relax in him and remember the works and words of God (Psalm 77:10-12).

> Remembering is an active tool to reignite our faith as we wait on God to move. Write down, speak out the promises He has made.

Remembering is an active tool to reignite our faith as we wait on God to move. Write down, speak out the promises he has made. As you do, your heart will fill with thanksgiving for the past and hope for the future. In between thanksgiving and hope is where we can find joy. We find joy in remembering this solid truth: while we wait, God works.

God is never idle. He takes no vacations. He is hard at work weaving together good plans and purposes that will exceed our greatest expectations (Romans 8:28; Ephesians 3:20). Be still and watch him work (Psalm 37:7). It is in waiting that we deepen our ability to trust God's love and goodness. While we wait, we can get to know God's heart and let him become our joy.

Joyful Truth

While we wait, God works. He is not going to hold back a single blessing from us, but rather give it to us at the right time (Psalm 84:11).

When waiting starts to drain our strength rather than fuel our hope and joy, let us remember to trust the Lord to answer our prayers in the right way, at the right time (Psalm 38:15). He hears the desperate cries of our hearts. Let us fix our hearts on foundational truths: God is love. God is faithful. God is good. He is not going to hold back a single blessing from us, but rather give it to us at the right time (Psalm 84:11). While we wait on him, he will renew our strength so we can persevere until he reveals his answer to our request (Isaiah 40:31).

Dear God, thank you for strengthening me and keeping me company while I wait. During seasons of waiting, remind me that the best is yet to come! Whenever I begin to feel anxiety rising in me, prompt me to stop and pray. Help me to always bring my desires to You, knowing that You always have my best at heart. As I trust in Your plan, fill me with thanksgiving, hope, and joy. Amen.

Reflect: Are you waiting in faith, expecting to see God's good and perfect gift or are you living in a place of frustration because He does not seem to be doing things your way in your time? How can you begin to honor God while you are waiting?

_____

_____

_____

_____

_____

_____

_____

_____

_____

_____

_____

_____

_____

_____

_____

_____

_____

_____

_____

_____

_____

_____

_____

_____

_____

_____

_____

_____

_____

_____

Joy of Authenticity

Read: 2 Timothy 1:3-10

"I'm reminded of your authentic faith, which first lived in your grandmother Lois and your mother Eunice. I'm sure that this faith is also inside you."
2 Timothy 1:5 CEB

Too often we hide our past hurts from people around us either because we are ashamed or because we fear rejection. We wear masks and hide the truth about ourselves to blend in. As a result, we often feel exhausted and depleted. Having to pretend to have it all together starves our hearts and leaves us empty. And it is not surprising, because we were created to be authentic. God wants us to have genuine community where we can be our true selves and be truly loved.

Without authenticity, how are pre-believers supposed to know that Jesus is real? That the Gospel has transforming power? That God's love truly never runs out or gives up on us? When we share stories about who we were and who we are becoming with others God gets the glory and lives are changed. When we are authentic, we become comfortable sharing how we need Jesus today, how we needed him yesterday, and how we will need him tomorrow. Authenticity is about humbly exposing our brokenness and flaws so that we can boldly proclaim God's grace. An authentic person is one who is both privately and publicly putting off the old self and, by God's grace, putting on the renewed self.

> Authenticity is about humbly exposing our brokenness and flaws so that we can boldly proclaim God's grace.

I believe this is what Timothy's mom and grandmother did. In the Bible, we read about Grandma Lois and mom Eunice, who shared with Timothy genuine faith (2 Tim. 1:5). Timothy saw these women authentically live a life for Christ. He saw when they made mistakes and he saw when they repented. Timothy saw when their faith was strong and weak. Their influence prepared this man to share the good news with many others. His biblically based upbringing was not only foundational for his relationship with God, but it was also vital to his usefulness in the Lord's service (1:6-7; 2 Timothy 3:14-16).

Joyful Truth

Being authentic brings joy because it creates a setting where we admit our imperfections while celebrating that God sees more than our imperfections.

Authentic is what we should be. Authenticity is an expression of the freedom Christ gives us. Oftentimes, we want people to only see all that is going right or when the mess has become a beautiful message. However, for true authenticity to bring people to Christ, people have to see when we do not have it all together, when we fall apart and when we struggle. Being authentic brings joy because it creates a setting where we admit our imperfections while celebrating that God sees more than our imperfections. Satan wants to use our past to paralyze us. God wants to use our past to propel us. The choice is ours. Let's be billboards for Christ, boldly displaying that we are under construction. Let people see the before, during, and after snapshots of our life.

Dear God, allow me to be authentic. Thank you for the scars and the story they tell. Be glorified by my authenticity. Please help me to point others to Your salvation today. Amen.

Reflect: How are you using your scars and authenticity to grow others in Jesus?

_____

_____

_____

_____

_____

_____

_____

_____

_____

_____

_____

_____

_____

_____

_____

_____

_____

_____

_____

_____

_____

_____

_____

_____

_____

_____

_____

_____

_____

Choose Joy

Read: Habakkuk 3:16-19

"Even though the fig trees have no blossoms, and there are no grapes on the vines; even though the olive crop fails, and the fields lie empty and barren; even though the flocks die in the fields, and the cattle barns are empty, yet I will rejoice in the Lord! I will be joyful in the God of my salvation!'"
Habakkuk 3:17-18 NLT

While there are beautiful, happy moments in life, there are also heartbreaking, gut-wrenching painful moments. That is simply a reality of life. We cannot choose the cards we are dealt, but we can choose how we play the hand. When we look at every challenge through the lens of joy, we are opening ourselves to accept that God can convert the pain into purpose. He can use our life challenges to lift us (and others) up. Now, let's be clear. Choosing joy is not about faking happiness. When we have a painful experience, we can feel a range of emotions. We should avoid, though, being stuck in despair.

The prophet Habakkuk was going through tough times. Extreme

poverty was coming. God had shown him the coming days when none of the crops or livestock—on which God's people depended—would be fruitful (3:17). When you read Habakkuk 3, you realize Habakkuk acknowledges the pain, disappointment, frustration, and fear of what was coming. Regardless of how bad the situation was, Habakkuk was determined to "rejoice in God." His focus was on God's character and power, rather than the circumstances. He could have joy because he was deeply anchored in the faithfulness of God. He chose joy in God because he knew that the God of his salvation would be faithful to

We can have joy in God when we place our confidence and faith in the greatness, goodness, and faithfulness of God.

see him through the worst. Even in the most horrible bad-to-worse situation, he was determined to focus on the bigness of God rather than the bigness of the problem.

Joyful Truth

We can choose joy in God because we know that the God of our salvation is faithful to see us through the worst.

How can we have joy in those moments when everything feels like it is falling apart; when God is silent, and we feel all alone, when it is one devastating news after another? Like Habakkuk, we can find joy in the trustworthiness of God's promises. He has promised to be with us (Hebrews 13:5), to strengthen us, to care for us, and to answer our prayers. We can have joy in God when we place our confidence and faith in the greatness, goodness, and faithfulness of God. Whatever our 'even though,' bad to worse situation—sickness, family crisis, financial trouble—we can rejoice as we put our hope in the God who provides the strength to walk in difficult places (v.19).

Dear God, Thank you that You are my "refuge and strength, a very present help in trouble" (Psalm 46:1). When I am faced with the difficulties of life, I can put my trust in You and cling tightly to your promise to work all things for good. When my world is turned upside down, be my joy. Though I can't yet see You in this difficult situation, I will praise You because I know You are there. Amen.

Reflect: What was your problem-upon-problem, bad to worse season? What was your response? How can you "rejoice in the Lord" during such times? What are some of God's promises from the Bible that can help you remember to trust God to see you through?

_____

_____

_____

_____

_____

_____

_____

_____

_____

_____

_____

_____

_____

_____

_____

_____

_____

_____

_____

_____

_____

_____

_____

_____

_____

_____

_____

_____

_____

ABOUT JOY

Joy Oguntimein, MPH is a Nigerian-American who calls the Washington Metropolitan area home. Joy tries to live by the motto 'Jesus. Others. You.' She believes if you live life following Jesus, walking with others, and being authentically you, then you will thrive. Joy is a positivity spreader who seeks opportunities to stir up the gifts and treasures within others to help them confidently and joyfully fulfill God's purpose for their life. Joy is a writer, worship leader, learning and development consultant, and pastor. She enjoys traveling and watching Marvel movies. Learn more at www.pocketfulofjoy.com

Made in the USA
Middletown, DE
05 November 2022

14223580R00066